LOOK OUT BEHIND YOU, SNOOPY

Selected cartoons from
HERE COMES THE APRIL FOOL
Volume 1

by CHARLES M. SCHULZ

FAWCETT CREST • NEW YORK

LOOK OUT BEHIND YOU, SNOOPY

This book, prepared especially for Fawcett Crest Books,
CBS Educational and Professional Publishing, a division of
CBS Inc., comprises a portion of HERE COMES THE
APRIL FOOL and is reprinted by arrangement with
Holt, Rinehart and Winston, Inc.

Contents of Book: PEANUTS® comic strips by
                  Charles M. Schulz
                  Copyright © 1979 United Feature
                  Syndicate, Inc.

ISBN: 0-449-24499-7

Printed in the United States of America

First Fawcett Crest Printing: April 1982

10   9   8   7   6   5   4   3   2   1

LOOK OUT BEHIND YOU, SNOOPY

HERE'S THE WORLD WAR I FLYING ACE SITTING IN A SMALL CAFE IN FRANCE

HE IS LONELY... HE IS DEPRESSED

HE REALIZES THAT HIS GIRL BACK HOME DOESN'T LOVE HIM ANY MORE..EVEN THOUGH SHE JUST SENT HIM A BOX OF COOKIES...

THEY'RE ALL FILLED WITH COCONUT!

BLEAH!

AAK!

HERE'S THE WORLD WAR I FLYING ACE WALKING ALONG A COUNTRY ROAD IN FRANCE...

HE NOTICES A BEAUTIFUL YOUNG GIRL APPROACHING FROM THE OPPOSITE DIRECTION...HE SPEAKS..

BONJOUR, SWEETIE!

SHE IS NOT IMPRESSED BY HIS FLUENT FRENCH

HERE'S THE WORLD WAR I FLYING ACE SOARING OVER THE FRONT LINES IN HIS SOPWITH CAMEL...

HE WAVES TO THE POOR BLIGHTERS IN THE TRENCHES BELOW

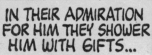

IN THEIR ADMIRATION FOR HIM THEY SHOWER HIM WITH GIFTS...

LIKE ROCKS!

HERE'S THE WORLD WAR I FLYING ACE STROLLING DOWN A COUNTRY ROAD...ONCE AGAIN HE SEES THE CHARMING FRENCH LASS..

QUICKLY HE CONSULTS HIS PHRASE BOOK... "I AM HAPPY TO MEET YOU"

ENCHANTÉ DE FAIRE VOTRE CONNAISSANCE

✳ SIGH ✳

EVERY DAY WHEN I WALK TO SCHOOL, I MEET THIS STRANGE CREATURE...

HE WEARS GOGGLES AND A WHITE SCARF

THAT'S MY BROTHER'S DOG...HE'S WEIRD...

YOUR BROTHER OR HIS DOG?

BOTH!

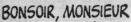

HERE'S THE WORLD WAR I FLYING ACE DOWN BEHIND ENEMY LINES WEARING ONE OF HIS FAMOUS DISGUISES

C MINUS ?!!

I WORK ALL NIGHT ON A PAPER, AND ALL I GET IS A "C MINUS"!

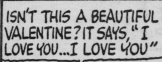

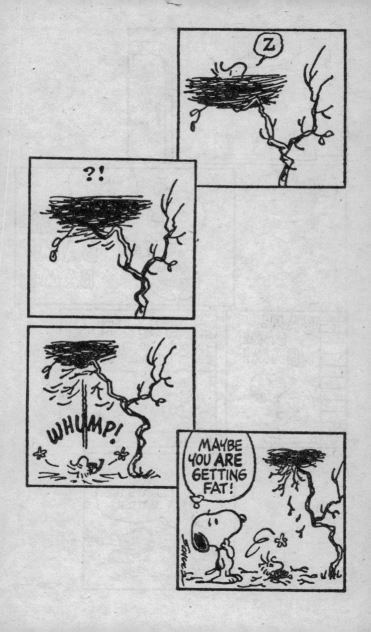

At first the cowboy rode his horse very fast.

Soon, however, he had to slow down.

The countryside was becoming too

hilllllllllly.

YOU'RE LUCKY, DO YOU KNOW THAT, BIRD? YOU'RE LUCKY BECAUSE YOU DON'T HAVE TO STUDY MATH!

YOU DON'T HAVE TO KNOW ABOUT RATIONALIZING THE DENOMINATOR AND DUMB THINGS LIKE THAT

YOU'RE REALLY LUCKY

$$\frac{7\sqrt{2}}{\sqrt{6}} \cdot \frac{\sqrt{6}}{\sqrt{6}} = \frac{7\sqrt{2 \cdot 2 \cdot 3}}{6} = \frac{7}{3}\sqrt{3}$$

SCHULZ

YOU KNOW WHAT I THINK YOU HAVE, SIR? YOU HAVE "MATH ANXIETY"

IF I ASKED YOU HOW MANY WAYS THAT NINE BOOKS COULD BE ARRANGED ON A SHELF, WHAT WOULD BE YOUR FIRST REACTION?

AAUGHH!

SEE? YOU HAVE "MATH ANXIETY"

GET THIS, CHUCK...SHE ASKS US HOW MANY ANGELS CAN STAND ON THE HEAD OF A PIN!

WHAT KIND OF A QUESTION IS THAT, CHUCK? HOW CAN YOU ANSWER SOMETHING LIKE THAT?

YOU CAN'T, PATTY...IT'S AN OLD THEOLOGICAL PROBLEM...THERE REALLY IS NO ANSWER...

THAT'S TOO BAD... I PUT DOWN, "EIGHT, IF THEY'RE SKINNY, AND FOUR IF THEY'RE FAT!"

INSCRUTABLE?

NO, MA'AM...I CAN'T SPELL INSCRUTABLE

YOU SAID, IF I TOOK PART IN THE SPELLING BEE, ALL I'D HAVE TO DO IS SPELL WORDS...

YOU DIDN'T SAY I HAD TO SPELL 'EM RIGHT!

WHAT'S THIS?

IT'S A BOOK ON HANDWRITING AND LETTERING

"AFTER PRACTICING THE CORRECT HAND MOVEMENTS WITH A PENCIL, YOU ARE NOW READY FOR PEN AND INK"

THE BLUE JAYS ARE AFTER YOU?

THEN YOU NEED ONE OF MY FAMOUS QUICK DISGUISES...

THERE! NOW THEY'LL THINK YOU'RE A RACCOON!

HEY, PITCHER, I'M A REPORTER FOR THE SCHOOL PAPER...

WHAT DO YOU THINK ABOUT WHEN YOU'RE STANDING OUT HERE ON THE MUD PILE?

THE MUD PILE?

I'LL PUT DOWN THAT HE WAS A LONELY LOOKING FIGURE AS HE STOOD THERE ON THE MUD PILE...

THE MUD PILE?

"THIS REPORTER HAS NEVER INTERVIEWED A WORSE BASEBALL TEAM"

"THE MANAGER IS INEPT AND THE PLAYERS ARE HOPELESS"

"WE WILL SAY, HOWEVER, THAT THE CATCHER IS KIND OF CUTE, AND THE RIGHT FIELDER, WHO HAS DARK HAIR, IS VERY BEAUTIFUL"

GOOD ARTICLE, HUH?

POW!

NOW I KNOW WHY
WE PLAY BASEBALL
IN THE SUMMER...

WHEN YOUR SHOES AND
SOCKS GET KNOCKED OFF
BY A LINE DRIVE, YOUR
FEET DON'T GET COLD!

THAT WAS SOME LINE DRIVE, CHARLIE BROWN... IT KNOCKED YOUR SHOESIES AND YOUR SOCKIES RIGHT OFF!

MAYBE WE SHOULD COUNT TO SEE IF YOU STILL HAVE ALL YOUR TOESIES...

GET OUT OF HERE!

JUST FOR THAT, HE CAN COUNT HIS OWN TOESIES!

BONK!

THAT'S FORTY-NINE FLY BALLS IN A ROW!

HOW COULD ANYONE DROP FORTY-NINE FLY BALLS IN A ROW?

THE SUN GOT IN MY EYES FORTY-NINE TIMES!

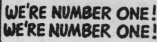

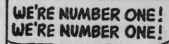

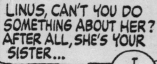

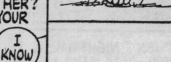

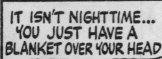

IT'S YOUR TURN.. ROLL THE DICE!

WHAT IF ROLLING THESE DICE LEADS ME TO A LIFE OF GAMBLING?

WHAT IF I CAN'T STOP? WHAT IF I BECOME A COMPULSIVE GAMBLER? WHAT IF I...

ROLLING DICE CAN RUIN YOU... SO CAN **NOT** ROLLING DICE!

THERE...I MOVED FIVE SQUARES..NOW, IT'S YOUR TURN...ROLL THE DICE!

IN THE TWENTY-EIGHTH CHAPTER OF EXODUS, IT TELLS OF 'URIM AND THUMMIM'.. SOME SCHOLARS SAY THESE WERE SMALL STONES LIKE DICE

THESE DICE WERE USED TO OBTAIN THE WILL OF GOD WHEN DECISIONS HAD TO BE MADE, AND...

ROLL THE DICE!

THAT'S A GOOD DECISION

IF YOU ROLL A SIX, YOU LAND IN THE WITCH'S DUNGEON

IF YOU ROLL A TWELVE, YOU GET TO GO TO "HAPPY PIGGYLAND"

I DON'T THINK I SHOULD ROLL THE DICE... I DON'T WANT TO RISK BECOMING A COMPULSIVE GAMBLER...

DON'T YOU WANT TO GO TO 'HAPPY PIGGYLAND'?!

LET ME SEE THAT BOOK! WHAT IS IT?

PHOOEY! I WOULDN'T READ THIS FOR ANYTHING!

NOT IN A MILLION YEARS! FORGET IT! NO WAY!!

LUCY HAS NO TROUBLE JUDGING A BOOK BY ITS COVER!

A YOUNGER BROTHER SHOULD KNOW HIS PLACE

A YOUNGER BROTHER SHOULD DO EVERYTHING HIS OLDER SISTER TELLS HIM TO DO, AND HE SHOULD DO IT FAST...

NOW, GO OUT TO THE KITCHEN, AND MAKE ME SOME HOT CHOCOLATE AND TWO TOASTED ENGLISH MUFFINS!

➤

THERE! HOW WAS THAT? I BROUGHT YOU JUST WHAT YOU ORDERED, AND I BROUGHT IT FAST!

YOU DIDN'T SALUTE!

WE COULD STILL RUN INTO SOME BAD WEATHER THIS TIME OF YEAR

I THINK YOU SHOULD BE WELL PREPARED LIKE I AM...

➤

A HIKE THROUGH THE WOODS IN THE SPRING CAN BE A JOY AND AN INSPIRATION...

IT CAN REVIVE YOUR SPIRITS, AND IT CAN..

..GET YOU INTO MORE TROUBLE THAN YOU EVER DREAMED OF IN YOUR WHOLE STUPID LIFE!

WHAT ARE YOU DOING HERE?
YOU'RE SUPPOSED TO BE
OUT SOMEWHERE SITTING
ON A BRANCH CHIRPING

THAT'S YOUR JOB...PEOPLE
EXPECT TO HEAR BIRDS
CHIRPING WHEN THEY WAKE
UP IN THE MORNING...

➡→

HOW CAN I DO A REPORT ON HANNIBAL, MARCIE? I'VE NEVER HEARD OF HIM!

RUN DOWN TO THE LIBRARY, SIR, AND LOOK HIM UP IN THE ENCYCLOPEDIA... THAT'S WHAT I DID..

MAYBE IT'LL SNOW TOMORROW, AND ALL THE SCHOOLS WILL BE CLOSED..

GOOD NIGHT, SIR!

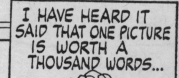

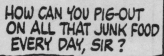
HOW CAN YOU PIG-OUT ON ALL THAT JUNK FOOD EVERY DAY, SIR?

LIFE IS MORE THAN CARROT STICKS, MARCIE

I'LL BET YOU'VE NEVER EVEN TRIED ONE, SIR

WHAT IS A STOMACH THAT'S EXPECTING A CHOCOLATE BAR GOING TO SAY WHEN IT GETS A CARROT STICK?

EXPLAIN TO IT THAT YOU'RE ALL PART OF THE SAME TEAM, SIR..IT'LL APPRECIATE BEING INVOLVED...

WHEN WE GET TO HIGH SCHOOL, I'M HOPING THAT WE'LL HAVE LOCKERS NEXT TO EACH OTHER

THAT WOULD BE AN ODD COMBINATION! HA HA HA HA HA!!

GET IT? LOCKERS HAVE COMBINATION LOCKS! AN ODD COMBINATION! GET IT?

MUSICIANS SHOULD NEVER TRY TO BE FUNNY

WHO IS THAT?

THAT'S BLACKJACK SNOOPY, THE WORLD FAMOUS RIVER BOAT GAMBLER...

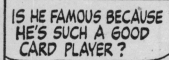

IS HE FAMOUS BECAUSE HE'S SUCH A GOOD CARD PLAYER?

NO, BECAUSE I HAVE TWO MUSTACHES!

SCHULZ

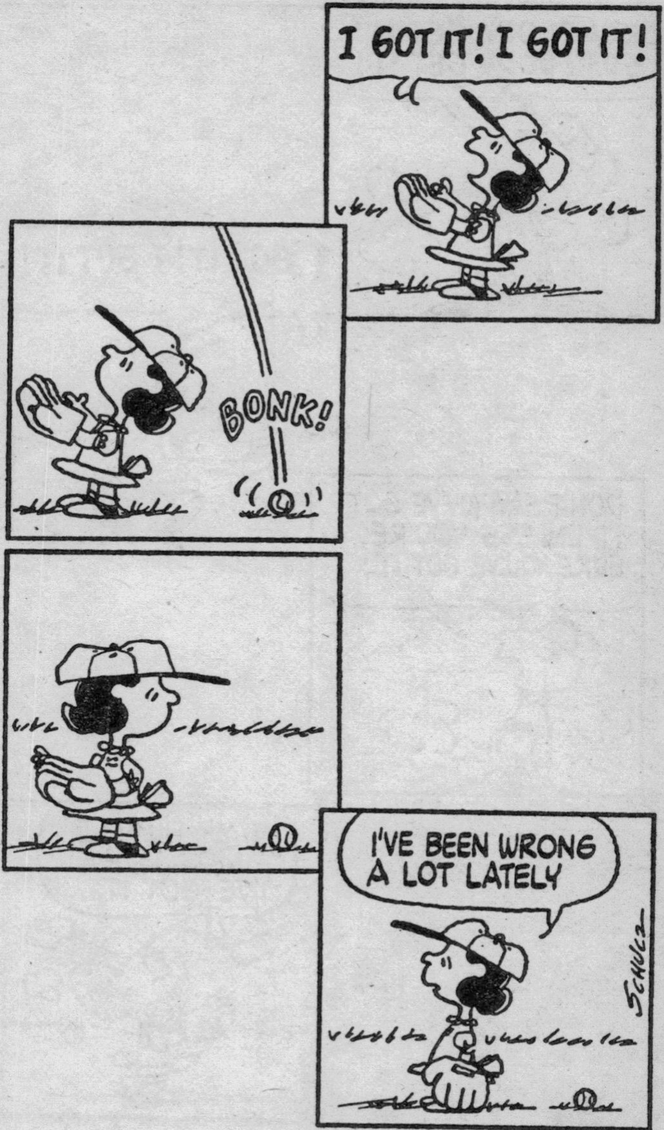
I GOT IT! I GOT IT!
BONK!
I'VE BEEN WRONG A LOT LATELY
SCHULZ

MORE PEANUTS®

☐ THIS IS THE BEST TIME OF DAY, CHARLIE BROWN
  (Selected cartoons from
  And a Woodstock in a Birch Tree, Vol. 3)   24485 $1.75

☐ BLAZE THE TRAIL, SNOOPY
  (selected cartoons from
  And a Woodstock in a Birch Tree, Vol. 2)   24452 $1.75

☐ YOU'RE OUR KIND OF DOG, SNOOPY
  (selected cartoons from
  And a Woodstock in a Birch Tree, Vol. 1)   24421 $1.75

☐ SING FOR YOUR SUPPER, SNOOPY
  (selected cartoons from
  The Beagle Has Landed, Vol. 3)   24403 $1.75

☐ SNOOPY, TOP DOG
  (selected cartoons from
  The Beagle Has Landed, Vol. 2)   24373 $1.75

☐ JOGGING IS IN, SNOOPY
  (selected cartoons from
  The Beagle Has Landed, Vol. 1)   24344 $1.75

☐ PLAY BALL, SNOOPY
  (selected cartoons from
  Win a Few, Lose a Few, Charlie Brown, Vol. 1)   23222 $1.75